I0148767

Elliot Christopher Cowdin

Report on Silk Manufactures

Elliot Christopher Cowdin

Report on Silk Manufactures

ISBN/EAN: 9783743309845

Manufactured in Europe, USA, Canada, Australia, Japa

Cover: Foto ©ninafisch / pixelio.de

Manufactured and distributed by brebook publishing software
(www.brebook.com)

Elliot Christopher Cowdin

Report on Silk Manufactures

REPORT

ON

SILK AND SILK MANUFACTURES,

BY

ELLIOT C. COWDIN.

UNITED STATES COMMISSIONER.

WASHINGTON:
GOVERNMENT PRINTING OFFICE.
1868.

CONTENTS.

SILK AND SILK MANUFACTURES.

SIR: The undersigned, Commissioner of the United States, and member of the Committee " on Raw Materials and Manufactures of great use or displaying remarkable skill or merit," to whom has been specially assigned the subject of silk and silk manufactures, respectfully submits the following Report:

Silk, by its characteristic qualities and unchangeableness, as well as by the richness and beauty of its appearance, is in relation to textile substances what gold is to metals.

It is of all filamentary substances that which gives the finest, most durable, and most elastic threads. Its tenacity is about equal to that of good iron; that is to say, a thread of silk of the same size will support nearly the same weight before breaking, and the textile matter affords an elasticity superior to that of the mineral substances.

Silk consequently unites the most brilliant properties with the most solid qualities. Its various, excellent, and advantageous characteristics have made it an object of research in all ages by the different nations of the world.

ANTIQUITY OF THE USE OF SILK.

China, even in our own day the most important country for the production of silk, appears to have been its cradle at the most remote epoch. The Chinese annals attribute to the Emperor Fau-Hi the merit of having employed silk in the manufacture of musical instruments of his own invention 3,400 years before the Christian era.

The Empress Si-Ling-Chi was the first to invent silk tissues, 2,650 years before our era, which invention contributed so immensely to the prosperity of her country that she was placed among the Chinese divinities, under the name of Sien Thsan,[1] and even now the Chinese empresses offer annually solemn sacrifices to her memory.

As it is the habit of the emperor of China once a year to plough the earth in order to add dignity and honor to agricultural pursuits, so in like manner the empress, by annually visiting the silk-worm nurseries and laboring with her own hands, encourages the production of this valuable commodity.

Two centuries before the Christian era the Chinese carried on a commerce in silk with Persia, Greece, and Italy. Their caravans or troops of dealers were protected by military settlements or colonies.

The generic name given to this precious material has remained

---

[1] This name means *the first promoter of silk industry*.

unchanged except with a slight modification of the word. In fact the French word *soie* or *silk* bears among them the name *sec.*

The Mongols name it *sirke*, the Mantchous *sirche.* The Russians designate it by the word *chek*, and the Greeks by *sez*, &c.

Notwithstanding the antiquity of the use of silk, its nature was for a long time unknown, and its importation into the west was of recent date compared to its high antiquity in Asia.

The history of the introduction of the first eggs of the silk-worm into Constantinople during the reign of the Emperor Justinian is well known.

The Chinese, determined to retain the monopoly of the silk industry, forbade the exportation of the eggs under penalty of death. They were, nevertheless, obtained A. D. 552, by two Persian monks, who had lived a long time in China as missionaries, and were acquainted with the rearing of silk-worms. Stimulated by the gifts and promises of the Emperor Justinian, they succeeded in conveying a large number of eggs concealed in hollow canes to Constantinople, where they watched their hatching and the development of the butterflies. The breeding of silk-worms spread, however, very slowly in Europe. The Moors imported them into Cordova about the year 910. Greece and Italy undertook it in the twelfth century; thence this branch of industry passed to Marseilles. At the commencement of the 14th century Pope Clement V introduced it into Avignon. Under Henry IV, Sully established a silk-worm nursery in the garden of the Tuileries. Louis XIV continued to encourage this enterprise in France, though with but slight success, so far as relates to the production of cocoons and the spinning of silk.

The weaving of silk goods with foreign thread had, on the contrary, already made marked progress in France, and had a great development, which it preserved even up to the revocation of the edict of Nantes, after which period the weaving as well as the spinning of silk lost ground considerably.

The emigrants carried this beautiful industry into England, Germany, and Switzerland, and raised the most active competition against France, where manufactures of silk remained in a languishing condition up to the close of the great revolution at the end of the last century, and until shortly before the return of peace to Europe.

RISE AND PROGRESS OF SILK INDUSTRY IN THE UNITED STATES.

America has not been insensible to the efforts made by other nations to appropriate to themselves the production of silk.

During the early periods of the colonization of Virginia, James I, on several occasions, advised with and encouraged the London Company in regard to the cultivation of the mulberry tree, and addressed a letter to the company in which he enjoined its members and exhorted the planters to apply themselves with diligence to the breeding of silk-worms, to establish silk-worm nurseries and spinning grounds, and to devote their activity rather to the production of this rich commodity than to that of tobacco, to which he manifested a profound aversion. Upon this advice, they planted a large number of mulberry trees, but collected little silk, in consequence of the difficulties resulting from the speedy dissolution of the London Company.

However, the culture of the mulberry was resumed in Virginia about the year 1651. The tree was indigenous in the colony, and the enterprise was so far advanced in 1660 that the coronation robe of Charles II was the product of the silk-worms of Virginia. But the steady advance of tobacco culture caused the business so to decline that it seems to have almost disappeared by the close of the century.

During the 18th century efforts were made to introduce silk husbandry into all the American colonies. It had been started, as early as 1718, with some success, in Louisiana, then under the dominion of Spain. The most strenuous exertions were directed to Georgia. Private gifts co-operated with acts of Parliament, and its settlers were stimulated by grants of land to cultivate the mulberry and raise silk-worms. In 1732, artisans, skilled in this industry, were sent over from Europe. The French emigrant who had charge of the business proved treacherous, and destroyed the machinery, eggs, and trees, and fled from Georgia.

The Italian who succeeded him was more trustworthy, and some raw silk was soon exported to Europe. In 1735 a beautiful robe was made in England of Georgia silk, which Queen Caroline wore on a great state occasion.

In 1740 the export of cocoons reached 1,000 pounds, and their product commanded the highest prices. A large silk establishment was soon erected in Savannah. The cocoons annually delivered to it, in the years from 1758 to 1766 inclusive, ranged from 10,000 pounds to 15,000 pounds, and in the latter year they reached 20,000 pounds. During the same period the annual export of raw silk ranged from 500 pounds to 1,000 pounds. At this period the silk culture was one of the most flourishing and profitable in the colony. But its success was of short duration. After 1766 the governmental bounties were withdrawn, and this industry began to droop. The storm of the revolutionary war prostrated it. After the peace, the planters of Georgia turned their attention to the growing of cotton, and silk culture utterly and finally disappeared.

The experiment in Georgia, its rise, progress, and decline, are the history of silk culture in all the colonies. Brief notices of some other colonies must suffice.

In South Carolina silk-growing was prosecuted before the Revolution, and for a time flourished. The mother of the celebrated Pinckneys carried some silk, produced on her plantation, to England, where it was woven into tissues. Gowns were made of it and presented by her to the mother of young George III, and to the elegant Earl of Chesterfield. But the same causes that uprooted the business in Georgia, destroyed it in Carolina. It passed away on the advent of cotton-raising.

Silk husbandry received early attention in Pennsylvania and New Jersey. The British government aided it by liberal bounties. Dr. Franklin, while in Europe in 1770, sent home mulberry cuttings, silkworms, eggs, &c., for distribution, and, with other influential citizens, gave it much encouragement.

In 1771 a silk establishment was set up in Philadelphia, which, during a series of years, received a large amount of cocoons. A lady of Lancaster county raised cocoons from which a piece of silk, fifty yards in length, was manufactured. From this a court dress was prepared for the Queen, who sent from Windsor Castle, in return, a handsome present to the fair donor on the banks of the Susquehanna.

Large mulberry groves flourished at Princeton, New Jersey, and cocoons of excellent quality were produced in encouraging quantities. But, as in the south, the convulsion of the Revolution, unusually severe in Pennsylvania and New Jersey, prostrated this branch of industry, and, though efforts were made after the peace to revive it, they were not specially successful.

Massachusetts and Connecticut took the lead in this enterprise in the east. It received the fostering support of the authorities. Governor Law, in 1747, appeared in a silk coat and stockings of home production. A few years afterwards President Stiles, of Yale College, officiated at Commencement in flowing robes of Connecticut silk. In 1770, Boston and New Haven vied with each other in raising cocoons, and in spinning, dyeing, and manufacturing raw silk.

A flourishing manufactory of sewing-silk was established at Mansfield, Connecticut, before the Revolution. Ipswich, Massachusetts, was at the same period noted for its silk products; while the largest and finest mulberry nursery in the country was growing at Northampton.

All these enterprises suffered by the blight which fell upon all industrial pursuits during the revolutionary war.

Silk husbandry and manufacturing had almost ceased to exist in the United States at the commencement of this century. Since then they have not kept pace with the advance in kindred pursuits.

Nevertheless, they have always been prosecuted to an encouraging extent in various parts of New England, New York, New Jersey, and Pennsylvania, as, for example, Mansfield, already referred to, has done a large business in sewing silks, and produced, in 1839, five tons of the raw material. Washington, Pennsylvania, always kept up the business. It was introduced into the State prison at Auburn, New York, in 1841, and the first year the product of sewing silk was about $13,000. It was steadily increasing in the country, when, some 25 years ago, its growth was checked by a disastrous speculative furor in the *morus multicaulis* shrub, which, for a few years, raged through the Union like an epidemic. The reaction fell heavily upon the whole business, covering it temporarily with odium and ridicule. It has since been slowly recovering from this season of delusion and folly.

In 1840 the product of silk raised in the United States was estimated at about 60,000 pounds, valued at $250,000. In 1844 it had increased to about 400,000 pounds, worth $1,500,000. By the census of 1850, when the effect of the speculative mania alluded to had culminated, the annual product was reported at only 14,763 pounds. Then it began to revive, and by the census report of 1860 it appears that the manufacture of sewing silk was carried on extensively in Connecticut, New Jersey, Massachusetts, Pennsylvania, and New York, the States being named in the order of the value of their products.

The annual production in those States, including tram, organzine, &c., was placed at upwards of $5,000,000.

Ribbons were made to a small extent, as were also silk stuffs. But, aside from sewing silks, the chief silk manufacture consisted of ladies' dress trimmings, coach laces, &c., of which the cities of Philadelphia and New York are reported as producing about $2,300,000. Since 1860, the business, in all its departments, has made steady progress, and the current period is more favorable than any previous one for its energetic prosecution.

Our country is specially fitted for silk culture. The experiments in Georgia and South Carolina proved that their soil and climate were peculiarly suited to it. May we not hope that, after a lapse of eighty-five years, it will be renewed in those States, and be prosecuted successfully not only there, but also in all the middle latitudes of the Union, whose rich soil, genial sun, and dry atmosphere are admirably adapted to the cultivation and manufacture of this beautiful and useful article?

But, though the possibility of the success of this kind of industry has been demonstrated in a great number of localities in America, it is probably to the Pacific coast that we are to look for its greatest triumph. Among the finest cocoons exhibited at the Exposition were specimens from California. They were perfect in form, and remarkable for their white, silvery hue. The soil in the valleys of California is proverbially fertile, and mulberry trees are produced of the richest and most luxuriant growth.

Its dry, warm, equable climate makes it vastly superior for silk husbandry to France or Italy. In European countries the rain and dampness destroy a much larger percentage of the grubs than on the Pacific coast. An intelligent and enterprising French emigrant, who is enthusiastically prosecuting this industry at San José, declares that the humidity and electricity of Europe destroy from 25 to 75 per cent. of the silk-worms, while under the dry, elastic skies of California few ever perish. These considerations in a measure compensate for the higher wages of American labor.

There are other savings in this industry as compared with its prosecution in Europe. In California there is no necessity for artificial heat to hatch the eggs. To transfer them from the cellar to the garret and expose them to the beating of the sun's rays is sufficient. Nor need the cultivator run the risk of the "baking" process, so liable to dim the lustre of the silk. The powerful rays of the sun for a few hours will stifle the chrysalis, render the cocoon ready for the spinner, and preserve the brilliancy of the material.

California eggs are already highly valued by foreign silk-growers. Cultivators are diffusing them along the Pacific coast. A considerable capital is invested in the silk business. The largest cocooneries are at Santa Barbara. An important experiment is now being made there by energetic parties, who have already 10,000 mulberry trees, and have produced the present year (1867) upwards of 300,000 cocoons of excellent quality.

An enterprising company is erecting an extensive factory at San José, to be furnished with all necessary machinery, including some forty looms, for producing taffetas in all colors and of the best qualities.

May we not hope that the day is not far distant when the plains that *slide down* from the western base of the Sierra Nevada will become as famous for beautiful silks as its gorges have long been for precious metals and its valleys are now becoming for cereals?

The nationality of the commission from which this report emanates must furnish the excuse for dwelling so long at the outset upon the subject of silk culture and manufacture in the United States. It will be resumed in brief terms near the close of the report. As germane to the American branch of this subject, it may be stated in this connection that silk culture was recently commenced in the republic of Ecuador. Its soil and climate are said to be wonderfully adapted to the growth of the mulberry and the rearing of the grub, especially in the neighborhood of Quito.

The first eggs were imported from France in 1859. The first exported to France was in 1865, where the eggs were highly esteemed, and were wholly exempt from the peculiar disease prevailing in Europe. Like its vegetation, silk culture in Ecuador can flourish the year round.

The food required by the worms is only half as much as in Europe, because of the superior richness of the leaves and the more favorable condition of the climate. The number of mulberry trees now growing in the republic is nearly a million. Labor is abundant and excessively cheap. The promoters of this enterprise in Ecuador indulge sanguine hopes of success. No doubt considerable portions of South America are well adapted to this department of industry.

REARING OF SILK-WORMS.

Numerous observations made by French and Italian scientific agriculturists and silk husbandmen show:

First. That the culture of the mulberry tree and the breeding of silkworms is possible up to a limit very far advanced northwards, a limit fixed by the frequent occurrence of a temperature of 77° Fahrenheit.

Second. The limit of the culture of the mulberry does not pass beyond that of the cultivation of the grape, and the culture of the former is possible wherever the latter will thrive.

Third. The mulberry can be raised upon the sides of the mountains of Europe up to the point where the mean temperature of the year is 49° Fahrenheit.

Fourth. Climates habitually stormy are not congenial to the breeding of the silk-worm.

Fifth. Places afflicted with fevers (proving the existence of marshy emanations) are pernicious to the silk-worm.

Sixth. This industry is to be considered rather as an adjunct to a large farm than as a chief occupation.

To these principles, given as the natural conditions necessary or hurtful to the industry of silk husbandry, are to be added the not less important questions of the price at which it returns from the hand of the workman in each locality, and of the abundance and scarcity of manual labor. We must, however, remark that the insufficiency of worms and their high price during more than ten years, in consequence of the malady of the precious grub in Europe, allow a remuneration sufficiently high to cover the expenses of the dearest hand labor, especially if we consider that the duration of care and attention which the harvesting of the worms demands does not exceed six weeks, counting from the day of hatching to a period after the warehousing of the cocoons, which latter, according to the best systems in use in Italy and France, can be reeled during the whole year.

PRODUCTION OF RAW SILK.

The production of the cocoons is essentially an agricultural industry, and the winding off the cocoons into raw silk may be considered as semi-manual and in part automatic. All the other transformations of the silk, from the throwing to the making of the stuffs, are entirely mechanical.

It can hardly be possible that henceforth the United States will not take a large share in the immense industrial and commercial movement to which silk has given rise in the world.

Certain countries, such as Italy and France and the oriental nations in general, employ themselves with all the transformations of silk, from the culture of the mulberry and the breeding of the worm to the manufacture of tissues.

England, (and others follow her example to a limited extent,) although not producing silk on her own soil, yet carries on a most important commerce in that article, by means of her colonies and powerful marine. She develops with equal activity the spinning or throwing of silk thread and the weaving of silk goods.

In a word, nations such as the United States, Switzerland, and Northern Germany, which are almost exclusively manufacturers, confine themselves to the transformation of silk bought in markets more or less distant.

The aptitudes of manufacturing nations change or are materially modified from time to time. Russia, for example, could, but recently, hardly be ranked among manufacturing nations. The people of that great empire are now making not only rapid progress in the industrial arts, but they have advanced in the south of Russia, on the Caucasus, even to the breeding of silk-worms.[1]

The production of the silk-worm in that country, since the annexation of trans-Caucasian Asia for example, has been three-fold, though the silk is far from being worked with the requisite care; it being generally irregular and suited only to the most common productions.

In 1865 this part of Russia exported nearly 30,000 kilograms, or 66,155 pounds,[2] representing a sum of about 1,560,000 francs, ($312,000,) that is to say, at the price of about 52 francs the kilogram, whilst that of France and Italy sold for at least double that price.

It is thought that the total silk production of Russia amounted to about 88,000 kilograms, or 194,054 pounds, estimated at a value of about 4,576,000 francs, ($915,200.) This result is far short of the limit which may be ultimately attained both in regard to quantity and price.

Germany and Switzerland have the same tendency, whilst France, the different States of Italy and Spain, in consequence of the scourge which attacked the production at its source some years ago, are becoming almost entirely manufacturing countries, and benefit India and the extreme east by their increasing wants.

The United Kingdom of Great Britain alone seems to profit by fluctuations so unfavorable to the rest of Europe, and even to America.

English ships go to collect in China, in Japan, at Calcutta, Bombay and elsewhere, the eggs or *graines*, cocoons, silk, and the *waste*, to sell again. After having first directly supplied her own manufactories, the surplus is disposed of to her neighbors in Europe; she thus profiting by the transport, warehousing, commissions, brokerage, &c.

Silk forms one of the principal articles of commerce in the business transactions of England with the extreme east.

The following table will show, as near as can be ascertained, the value of raw silk produced annually in the various countries of the earth, and its vast importance as an element of national wealth:

Asia..	$141,000,000
Europe...	73,480,000
Africa..	220,000

---

[1] The culture of the mulberry tree. the introduction of which into Russia dates from the period of Peter the Great, remained without any great results up to the commencement of the present century.

[2] The metrical system being in use in most of the countries from which we have derived our information, and constantly tending to extend itself more and more, especially since the international conference at Paris, we have thought it useful and proper to retain in part, for the numbers cited, the franc as the unit of money and the kilogram as the unit of weight.

Oceanica	$120,000
America	80,000
Total	**$214,900,000**

These amounts may be divided as follows, viz:

Chinese empire	$81,200,000
Japanese empire	17,000,000
Persia	5,000,000
The island of Asia Minor	5,200,000
Syria	1,800,000
Turkistan (in China)	400,000
Turkistan (independent, in Asia)	1,400,000
Corean archipelago	100,000
France	25,600,000
Italy	39,200,000
Turkey in Europe	7,000,000
Spain and Portugal	3,200,000
Pontifical States	1,300,000
Greece, Ionian islands	840,000
Morocco, Algeria, Tunis, Mediterranean coast	300,000
Basin of the Danube, Austria, Bavaria, Servia, Hungary	1,280,000
India	24,000,000
America	80,000
Total	**$214,900,000**

These figures have been greatly reduced during the last few years, as far as concerns the production in Europe. The difference, however, was made up by the quantities received from China, India, Japan, and the Levant.

But those *erotic* silks are far from being as highly esteemed or as valuable as those of Europe.

The modification in the relative value of silk which has taken place during a century is worthy of note.

A century ago nearly all the silk, or at least five-sixths of the quantity manufactured by French fabricants, came from foreign countries, from the Levant, from Persia, Sicily, Italy, and Spain.

The other sixth only was produced in the south of France. The mean price of French silk was 15 francs the *lirre*, or 30 francs the kilogram, (2½ pounds.) Exotic silks were much dearer. The most common foreign raw silk, that of Greece, then brought 120 francs the kilogram; China and India silks, 240 francs; and that of Italy was valued at from 500 to 600 francs.[1] But by degrees French silk improved to such an extent

---

[1] These are the prices as published in the price current of the Amsterdam market, where at that period the greatest quantity of foreign silk was sold.

that, in the early part of this century, the price advanced to 70 francs the kilogram. This rate was maintained almost without variation up to the year 1840; while foreign products were depreciated to such a degree, that the very best quality from the Levant and from Persia sold at 40 francs and the waste at 32 francs.

Italy during this period maintained the elevation in its prices, on account of the very excellent quality of its silks. That was nevertheless surpassed by the French silks, which finally rose from the last to the first rank, which they still maintain.

The raw silks of France, of the first quality, at a later period brought 150 francs, while those of the best kind from Italy realized hardly 100 francs. These results are due entirely to the progress in French manufactures, which has hardly contributed to the extraordinary development of the silk industry that has occurred in that country.

This specialty of silk industry has given to France the importance that the cotton industry has to England.

In this connection it may be profitable to give a rapid sketch (so far as data will permit) of the progressive development of silk culture and manufacture in the principal countries of Europe and Asia. The amounts are given in round numbers, and though obtained from trustworthy sources may be liable to some corrections.

In 1789 France produced 1,000,000 pounds of raw silk. Near the close of the century she consumed about 1,200,000 pounds of silk thread, from which she manufactured from $3,000,000 to $4,000,000,[1] (15,000,000 to 20,000,000 of francs.) Of this she purchased about $1,400,000 (7,000,000 of francs) from other countries. The stock of stuff goods consequently amounted to from $4,400,000 to $5,400,000, (22,000,000 to 27,000,000 francs,) of which France exported about one-half to foreign countries.

In 1812 France produced 600,000 pounds of raw silk and 340,000 pounds of organzine, valued at $5,000,000. The same year she imported 900,000 pounds, valued at $6,750,000.

In 1820 it is estimated that French manufacturers transformed $10,000,000 (50,000,000 francs) of materials, of which one-half was furnished by the southern departments. The goods produced from these materials represented a value of more than $20,000,000, (100,000,000 francs,) of which $14,000,000 (70,000,000 francs) were consumed at home, and $6,000,000 (30,000,000 francs) were exported.

As first in importance we begin with France.

PROGRESSIVE DEVELOPMENT OF SILK INDUSTRY.

FRANCE.

In 1812 the silk looms in seven of the principal towns of the empire numbered 27,000. In 1824 Lyons alone had nearly 25,000. In 1839 the number in Lyons had increased to 40,000, and in the whole kingdom to

---

[1] Dollars at *gold* valuation in all cases.

85,000, employing about 170,000 workmen. In the latter year the entire production was estimated at $46,300,000.

In 1850 the business had largely increased. The value of raw silk grown in the kingdom was $28,000,000, (140,000,000 francs.) **The capital employed, $50,000,000,** (250,000,000 francs,) the amount imported being $22,000,000.

The silk goods produced were valued at $75,000,000, (375,000,000 francs,) of which about one-third were consumed at home and two-thirds exported.

In 1855 the value of silk goods sold was **estimated at $106,500,000,** of which about $26,500,000 was imported. The home consumption was $35,000,000, and the export was about $71,500,000. The number of silk looms in the empire was about 225,000. **The number** of persons engaged in this industry was upwards of half a million.

In 1860 the value of French silks amounted to upwards of $140,000,000, (700,000,000 francs,) and yet this was not sufficient to supply the demand. France purchased **in foreign** countries $40,000,000, (200,000,000 francs,) chiefly of piece goods, velvets, and ribbons. Of this $180,000,000 France exported about **$110,000,000,** (550,000,000 francs.)

These totals **were reduced at** the outbreak of **the** American **rebellion.** France restricted **to a marked degree** her purchases **of** silks. **The United** States purchased from **France of silk** tissues alone, in 1859, $27,600,000, (138,000,000 francs;) in 1860, **$20,800,000,** (104,000,000 francs,) but in 1861 only $5,000,000, (25,000,000 **francs.)**

Subsequently the business increased, the Lyons exports of silks to the United States in 1865 amounting to **$9,900,000,** and in 1866 to $6,000,000.

Though the rebellion has been **suppressed, the fiscal measures** resulting therefrom still have their effect upon the silk husbandry and manufacture of France, operating as they do at the same period with the scarcity of indigenous silk, and the prevalence of mysterious disease among the silk-worms, which has by no means disappeared, and **to which** special reference will be hereafter made.

GREAT BRITAIN.

When the **Duke of Parma sacked the city of** Antwerp, in 1585, its silk artificers fled to England, carrying with them their experience and skill in this novel branch of industry. It was encouraged by the English government, but the humid climate being unfavorable to the rearing of the grub, it was not specially successful.

On the revocation of the edict of Nantes, in 1685, some 75,000 of the most skilful artisans of France took refuge in Great Britain, among whom were a large body of silk weavers, who settled in Spitalfields, (then a London suburb,) and under the fostering care of the Crown they and their children plied their vocation with success for a century and more, some of their descendants remaining in the same locality to this day.

For 30 or 40 years after immigration England was wholly dependent on foreigners for organzine silk thread, but in 1718 Mr. Lombe, an English capitalist, visited Piedmont disguised as a common laborer, took sketches of silk-throwing machinery in use there, and on his return erected an extensive mill at Derby, which produced more than 3,000,000 yards of organzine per day.

For many years raw silk was largely imported. Acts of Parliament were passed from time to time stimulating its manufacture, and the business was steadily advancing, when, in 1764, on account of low wages, scarcity of work, and the preference shown for French silks, the weavers of Spitalfields and the silk operatives of other localities assembled, in a tumultuous manner, and petitioned Parliament for the total prohibition of foreign-wrought silks. The commotion was kept alive by combinations of operatives for several years, till, in 1772, it broke into open riots, which convulsed London many days, the final result being the passage of prohibition laws, which after trial proved unsatisfactory.

This system of prohibitory legislation continued till 1824. A high English authority has declared that "the manufacturer, depending upon the protection of parliamentary restrictions on foreign competition rather than on his own skill and exertions, was not anxious to discover and introduce improvements into the manufacture." And he states that " since the change of system the imports of the raw material and the exports of the manufatured article have rapidly increased." In 1825 the English silk looms numbered about 24,000; in 1855 they had increased to more than 110,000, consuming about 5,500,000 pounds of thrown silk, and producing goods to the value of near $45,000,000, besides a considerable amount of spun silk, and goods of which silk constituted a part.

In 1855 England consumed of her own silk manufactures more than $35,000,000, while she imported about $20,000,000. In 1860 the value of her silk manufactures was estimated at some $90,000,000. On account of the extreme dampness and chilliness of her climate, (of which mention has been made,) she raises no silk-worms, but imports the raw material.

In 1856 the value of her imports of raw silk was (omitting fractions) $32,000,000, and in 1867 $58,000,000. It fell off in 1858 on account of the "panic," but again revived. Nearly one-half the amount of the raw material came from China, and a large share of the balance from her East India possessions.

During the three years just mentioned England imported $1,300,000 of thrown silk, more than one-half being from France, and nearly one-third from China.

In 1860 the British consumption of raw and thrown silk was 9,420,417 pounds; in 1861, 8,125,982 pounds; in 1862, 9,706,202 pounds; in 1863, 8,182,645 pounds; in 1864, 7,541,578 pounds; in 1865, 6,492,720 pounds; and in 1866 it was but 5,273,767 pounds.

In 1823 Great Britain exported of silk goods only $702,000; in 1844 it exported $3,682,000; in 1856, $14,800,000; in 1858, $11,950,000; in 1861, $11,560,900; in 1865, $10,886,000.

Thus we see that this great manufacturing nation, notwithstanding by its uncongenial climate deprived of the capacity to successfully produce the raw material, has long prosecuted a large business in the transformation of this beautiful article, though now seriously checked in many branches of its silk industry by the effect of the recent treaty with France.

What an instructive lesson is thus taught to the citizens of our country, where everything combines to render the prosecution of this industry pre-eminently successful.

OTHER EUROPEAN COUNTRIES.

Italy was early famous for its silk culture and manufactures. In Milan and vicinity, in the year 1800, about 2,000,000 pounds of raw silk were said to have been collected. In 1825 the quantity was estimated at 2,700,000 pounds, valued at $10,000,000; in 1858 at 5,400,000 pounds, worth $30,000,000. In 1825 Piedmont produced about 1,500,000 pounds of raw silk of the very highest quality. In the same year Tuscany, Naples, the Romagna, and Calabria produced 1,500,000 pounds, also excellent in quality. In 1851 an Austrian official document stated the productions in the Austrian dominions of Italy at $21,700,000 in raw silk, and $14,200,000 in manufactured silks. In 1855 the total of both kinds of silk in the whole Italian peninsula was stated at upwards of $60,000,000. A considerable portion is consumed at home, and the remainder exported chiefly to Germany, France and England.

Spain produced in 1842 about 2,000,000 pounds of raw silk, three-fifths of which was raised in Valencia. About 400,000 pounds were manufactured at home, and the rest exported. The Spanish cocoons are excellent, but much of the reeling is defective. Valencia silks, where great care has been taken in the manipulation, are famous for their magnificence.

In Prussia silk manufacture is rapidly increasing. The number of looms in 1831 was 9,000; in 1837, 14,000; in 1855, 25,000; and in 1865 not less than 40,000. In the Exhibition were superb silks, velvets, velvet ribbons, black silk ribbons, mixed and unmixed silk fabrics of various descriptions, from Crefeld, Elberfeld, Viersen and vicinity. The waters in that locality, especially those of the Wipper, hold in solution salts specially adapted to secure permanency and brilliancy to the colors employed in manufacture.

Austria is engaged somewhat extensively in silk manufacture, but since she relinquished her Italian dominions this industry has doubtless received a check.

The product of Switzerland in 1858 was placed at $20,000,000. The "Collective Exhibition of the Zurich Manufacturers" of black and colored silks, plain and figured, and the "Collective Exhibition of the Basle Silk Ribbon Manufacturers," as shown in the Exposition, evince the progress and perfection to which Swiss skill in silk industry has now attained.

Russia has already been alluded to. After France and England, the nations that come in the order of their importance in respect to silk manufactures are Switzerland, Prussia, Austria, Italy, and Spain. France maintains a great superiority over all in her rich and artistic productions; but in plain goods, and those of a secondary quality, she finds serious rivalry in British, Swiss, and German industry. Switzerland is becoming remarkable for her activity, her constant progress, and her improvements in material interests.

In a subsequent part of this report the occasion will be embraced to examine the improvements she brought to the Exposition, since there is a great analogy between the situation and industrial genius of that republic and the social and manufacturing condition of the United States.

ASIATIC COUNTRIES AND AFRICA.

China raises, manufactures, consumes, and exports a vast amount of silk. It is impossible to estimate the quantity consumed at home. A high authority declares that, of her 400,000,000 of people, a large proportion, excepting the lowest classes, are clad more or less in silk fabrics. She exported to England alone, in 1858, nearly 10,000,000 pounds. In the East India Company's possessions the product is large. In 1857 they exported to England about 4,500,000 pounds. Persia produced great quantities, much of which is consumed at home. The amount raised in Syria and Asia Minor is some 2,500,000 pounds per annum, of which a large share is exported to France and England. Reference to other Asiatic countries, of inferior importance in this particular, is omitted.

Silk has long been produced in small quantities along the African shores of the Mediterranean. England imports some of the raw material from Egypt, but the greatest share of the productions of the Nile region is consumed at home. Tripoli produced in 1842 about 130,000 pounds. The islands of Cyprus and Crete raised in 1856 some 50,000 pounds.

SPECIALTIES OF SILK INDUSTRY.

The labor in silk comprises seven distinct branches, forming as many different industries, even when a single manufacturer conducts several in one establishment. These specialties are—

1. The breeding or rearing of silk-worms, called in France the art of the *magnanier*, (or silk-worm breeder.) This word comes from *magnan*, the name given to the grub of the white mulberry in the south of France.

The appellation *magnanerie*, or silk-worm nursery, is given to the locality where the worms are hatched, fed, and attended to from their birth till they have formed their silky envelope or cocoon.

These silk-worm nurseries are generally established in localities or countries favorable to the cultivation of the mulberry tree, of whose leaves, and white fruit especially, the worm is particularly fond; and also where the temperature is regular and moderate. Nevertheless, this last condition is not indispensable. It is replaced artificially by special means of warming and ventilating, so as to maintain at will, constantly, the temperature between 70° and 75° Fahrenheit, and thus be able to breed numerous little grubs; (one ounce, or 30 grams, contains about 40,000, while from 20 ounces 800,000 have been obtained at a time, in the same place.) The result is arrived at chiefly by watchfulness in ventilation, in removing the vitiated air **and replacing it by pure air.**

The art of the silk-worm **breeder embraces** what is called "the fabrication of the *graine*," or, more correctly, of the eggs to be used **in the** reproduction. The cocoons destined for this function are the only ones whose chrysalis or grub is allowed to be transformed into the butterfly. These are **moistened,** and then the grub opens one of the lengthened extremities of the cocoon, and issues from it.

Then **the** grubs are collected by pairs, male and female, to permit fecundation before the laying of the eggs. These *fecondés*, suspended on paper or cloth, are subsequently put aside until the following spring, in an atmosphere of even temperature, and sufficiently low, like that of cellars.

This part of the art of the breeder, so simple in appearance, demands special knowledge and great care, particularly at this time, when it is so difficult to procure **eggs free from** the epidemic now raging among the silk-worms.

2. The second **specialty in this** industry is the *filature*, or reeling **of the** silk from the cocoons into the threads known as raw silk, and composed of fibres of a certain number of cocoons according to the size of the thread required. It is a most delicate untwisted product, but wanting in lustre on account of its containing some 25 per cent. of gum.

3. The throwing of silk, **or the** process of putting the raw **silk into the** threads required for the different kinds of weaving.

It is at the throwing that the threads are formed that figure **so conspicuously** at the Exposition, and also in commerce, under the **names of** simples, trams, and organzines. There are also other kinds **of thrown** silk, known as *marabouts, grenadines, crêpe, soie ondée,* &c., which **are** twisted differently from trams and organzines, for special purposes.

Let us look for a moment at the comparative value of each of these denominations. The singles are the raw silk after the first twist. The tram, or woof, is obtained by the union of two or more threads of raw silk, slightly twisted. The organzine, from which in general is made the warp, is the result of two singles twisted together.

A product of peculiar nature, frequently used in the manufacture of trimmings, is the *fil guipé*. It is composed of one or more straight threads, around which is rolled a spiral thread, the interior being generally of indifferent material, and the thread rolled around is composed of silk, gold, or **silver.**

4. **The** dyeing constitutes **an important specialty, requiring the great-** est possible delicacy and **skill, pure water being essential to success.**

5. The preparation of the **threads for the loom** is another separate and essential branch, requiring **care and attention.**

6. The **weaving** embraces **in itself alone several subdivisions, namely,**

the weaving of plain and cut silk goods; the weaving of velvets of figured stuffs more or less rich; the knitting of various articles and the fabrication of silk *blondes* or laces.

THE SPINNING OF WASTE SILK.

7. The preceding processes yield a certain quantity of *waste*, varying with the nature of the operations and the qualities of the products.

This waste is in its turn transformed from the raw state, where, after having been cleaned from the gummy matter, chiefly by mechanical means, it presents a close analogy to the strippings and windings of cotton and combed wool.

These processes are the basis of great industries which flourish in England and on the continent.

The threads thus produced vary in value from 30 to 60 francs the kilogram, according to their fineness and quality.

These branches of industry are now carried on to some extent by American manufacturers.

EXAMINATION OF THE POSITION OF EACH OF THESE INDUSTRIES, AND THEIR PROGRESS AS MANIFESTED IN THE EXPOSITION.

In the art of silk-worm breeding the question of first importance consists in the means of obtaining the *graines*, or eggs. Good eggs bear an exorbitant price. They are worth at the rate of 300 francs the kilogram, and still they cannot always be produced guaranteed against the prevailing malady, except from Japan.

The States of South America appear to enjoy the same immunity. At the commencement of the prevailing epidemic, (about the year 1846,) other countries furnished healthy eggs, but their exemption did not continue after the second or third generation. Thus it is that the United States have been led to put all silk-producing countries under contribution.

Will the eggs of Japan and of South America, at the present time so much sought after, escape this degeneracy, of which, despite the numerous investigations, we as yet do not know the cause?

But if the cause remains concealed, the preventive means begin to be more clearly established.

The following method is generally admitted and recommended by men recognized as the most competent judges, and since it is the combined result of great experience and observation, it will be read with interest in all countries which desire to encourage the culture of the silk-worm:

It is of great importance to choose for reproduction cocoons of the largest size, and those the most successfully reared and least affected with the malady during the course of their development. These cocoons are recognized by the regularity of their form, the roundness of their extremities, the fineness of grain on the surface, and the solidity and thickness of the layers or silky envelopes.

The male cocoons differ from the female by their shape and size. The former are smaller than the latter, and present a cavity upon their back. The latter are larger, presenting the figure of an olive or the egg of a small bird.

The color of these cocoons ought to be of a golden yellow after collecting, and should exhibit no spot or stain of any kind.

In the same breed, the heaviest cocoons are in general those which offer the greatest chance of affording the best reproductions. Then, after having put a certain number of male cocoons on one side and of female on the other, weigh both parts to find the average weight of each, and every time that this average weight is exceeded there is a presumption that excellent cocoons are obtained for reproduction, all other things being equal.

It is, however, necessary to remark that, as one part of the cocoons contains sometimes the same gross measurement, it should not be confounded with the normal cocoons. Cocoons of an exceptional bulk are in general the result of two grubs united under the same envelope. Their product is known under the name of "doubles," or "*douppions,*" or twin threads.

This sort of product is always inferior, as much because the beds or envelopes are almost invisible, as because the association in the work indicates a weakness in the subject.

Notwithstanding all the attention and care given by the breeder to prevent the production of doubles, and sometimes even of triples, he must inevitably expect to find a certain proportion of those, the value of which is hardly one-third the price of the normal product.

There was exhibited in the Exposition an apparatus contrived by an Italian silk husbandman, designed to prevent these *douppions* in the breeding of worms.

The apparatus consists in an arrangement of cells made of very light wood, each one of which has only the bulk necessary for a single grub. When these come to their full development, ready to spin their cocoon or boll, instead of preparing heath, shrubs, or other kinds of shelter or supports against which the worms are to spin, this kind of cells is supplied where each insect has its own separate case, which prevents two or any greater number from uniting to make a defective product.

The Italian exhibitor is endeavoring to bring into general use this system of isolation or cellular breeding.

The system presents, according to the inventor, other advantages, by the facility which it offers in the choice of the best reproducers, and by preventing the coupling between grubs of the same family, consanguinity having been considered as one cause of the rapid deterioration of the breed.

When the coupling has been accomplished, the females are removed and made to lay, each in the cell reserved for her, in such a way as to be able to weigh separately the eggs of each laying.

This weight is not to be inferior to a certain ascertained proportion, for the eggs would then be evidently bad. In order that they may offer good chances of success, each laying should weigh at least 60 or 70 grams, (per kilogram of cocoons,) each gram to contain 1,350 to 1,500 eggs on an average.

THE SILK-WORM AND ITS VARIETIES.

THE COMMON SILK-WORM, *(Bombyx Mori.)*

The common silk-worm and the species mostly in use, and which produces by far the best silk, is born in the spring, ordinarily about the middle of May. It feeds on the leaves of the mulberry tree and attains its full growth in about six weeks.

During that period it changes its skin four times, and according to M. de Quatrefages, of the French Institute, increases its weight 72,000 times. Early in July, having reached its full development, it establishes the workshop of its wonderful manufacture.

Placed in a comfortable and secure position, it proceeds to envelop itself in a cocoon formed by a filament of exceedingly fine silk, emitted from the stomach of the insect. It soon disappears in the centre of the cocoon or silken envelope, and, after about 72 hours of unremitting labor, produces a thread ordinarily not less than 1,600 yards in length.

In that chosen retreat the silk-worm again sheds its skin, for the fifth time, but the insect which comes out is no longer a silk-worm, but a chrysalis—bearing but slight resemblance to the worm. After two weeks or more, according to the temperature, the skin of the chrysalis opens, and, changing for the last time, it becomes a butterfly, lays some hundreds of eggs, and dies.

Besides the *Bombyx Mori*, there are other species of silk-worms that merit a brief notice, and particularly the following:

CASTOR-OIL PLANT SILK-WORM, *(Bombyx Arrindia.)*

This species of silk-worm is a native of Bengal and of British India. It lives, both in its wild and its domesticated condition, upon common castor-oil plants and other vegetation. It was but lately introduced into Europe by means of a few living cocoons imported into Malta. Their propagation was not only successful, but was continued in Italy, whence many were sent to France and the Canary islands.

Wherever the castor-oil plant grows spontaneously, as in Algiers, Brazil and Rio de la Plata, the efforts to raise this species of silk-worm have been crowned with success. Its cocoons cannot be reeled in the ordinary way, but they furnish a staple which, when spun into threads, produces fabrics of good suppleness and durability, though almost destitute of lustre.

AILANTHUS SILK-WORM, *(Bombyx Cynthia Vera.)*

This kind of worm is indigenous to the temperate regions of China, where it lives mainly on the ailanthus. It has long been cultivated by the Chinese in the open air, and produced an elongated cocoon of a reddish shade, furnishing a kind of *bourre de soie*, from which is made a very strong and durable tissue.

This silk-worm was introduced into Europe for the first time in 1857, and into France in 1858, where the first successful rearing of it is chiefly due to Madame Drouyn de Lhuys.

But it is to M. Guerin Ménéville, who, under the patronage of the Emperor, experimented extensively and with success, that belongs the credit of having given to this silk its growing importance and industrial value.

THE TUSSEH SILK-WORM, *(Bombyx Milita.)*

This notable insect lives in a wild state in Bengal, and in the hot regions of India, in the woods, where the inhabitants go to gather the cocoons, which are remarkable for their size and form. Its favorite food is the leaves of the jujube tree. Efforts have been made repeatedly to reproduce it in France, but in vain. The cocoons of this insect produce a fine and brilliant silk, and very strong, known in India as *Tusseh*, of which large quantities are exported to Europe.

THE WILD SILK-WORM OF JAPAN, *(Bombyx Yama May.)*

This worm, raised from eggs sent from Japan by the consul-general of France at Yeddo, has been successfully reared. The oak leaf and trees of the same kind are its only nourishment. It does not require great heat, and is easy to raise. Its cocoon, of a greenish yellow, is formed like that of the ordinary silk-worm, and can be reeled into a beautiful silk.

BOMBYX CECROPIA.

This description of worms, indigenous to the temperate regions of North America, is found principally in the Carolinas, Louisiana and Virginia.

In its uncultivated state it lives upon the elm, the willow, and other trees. It produces a large cocoon of a loose texture and coarse silk.

At the Exposition there was a collection of silk-worms in their different stages. A quantity of eggs, of mulberry leaves, and all that relates to the rearing of the silk-worm, were also displayed there.

The silk-worm is tender and delicate. The experiences of the last twenty years have proven that it is liable to epidemics, that rage with peculiar violence and fatality.

THE SILK-WORM MALADY AND THE REMEDIES PROPOSED.

During the period in which the disease in question has attacked the silk-worms, great research and the most minute study have been made to ascertain the cause.

Some have ascribed this calamity to the mulberry; others have compared it to a species of Asiatic cholera, or an epidemic analagous to the cattle distemper from which England and Germany have suffered so much within the last few years.

Others have asserted that the breeder had gradually departed from and neglected those healthful traditions and maxims so essential to be observed in the breeding and rearing of such delicate creatures.

The breeder, perceiving that he could abridge the period of rearing by raising the temperature of the nursery, prematurely matured unhealthy broods, and thence there arose numerous accidents, because by raising the temperature the appetite was forced, which caused derangements in the animal economy.

These different causes, more or less vague and indeterminate, may have contributed to the development of the epidemic. However, the theory of disease in the mulberry is hardly admissible, considering that it has been demonstrated that worms of different breeds or races, nourished by the leaves of the same tree, have experienced different fates. Some succeeded, the others were attacked by the disease and perished; therefore the food in these cases was innocent of the effect.

In the difficulties by which we find ourselves involved in endeavoring to determine the cause of the malady, we have only to seek out the character and seat of the evil, to be able *a priori* to reject infected subjects.

After numerous investigations by eminent men, certain spots or bodies of peculiar form and appearance were discovered, with the aid of the microscope, in the very tissues of the diseased worms at the bottom of their digestive canal, evidently foreign to their organization, and in quantities proportionate to the violence of the disease. To these little spots or bodies the name of *corpuscules* was given. They are oval, transparent, smaller than the globules of the human blood, and resemble the globules of certain fermentations.

Widely different theories prevail in regard to these corpuscules and the remedies required for their eradication. The distinguished savant M. Pasteur has come to the conclusion that it is an organic, constitutional affection of the insect, to destroy which either a specific remedy must be found, or else all the conditions favorable to the production of the corpuscules must be avoided, either by obtaining eggs from countries exempt from the malady, or by allowing none but healthy insects to propagate. He has demonstrated that contact between healthy and infected worms does not impart the disease; while, on the other hand, the absorption of a few corpuscules by feeding upon leaves washed with corpusculous water causes the epidemic to spread with incredible rapidity.

M. Pasteur is of the opinion that search must be made for the corpuscules in the chrysalis, and he developes a very ingenious method for facilitating the discovery.

He recommends the immediate destruction of all insects known to be infected, and the separation from them of the healthy ones, and enjoins the utmost cleanliness as an essential condition for the extirpation of the disease in a silk nursery.

M. Béchamp, who has devoted great patience to the investigation, propounds the theory that the disease is parasitic, and that the parasite is of a vegetable nature of the order of fermentations, and that remedies like creosote will arrest if not destroy the development of these vegetable corpuscules.

His mode of application is to wash the eggs in a solution of creosote, or diffuse an impregnating vapor through the rooms of the silk-worm nursery. Suffice it to say, that the methods recommended by each of these gentlemen for the extermination of the disease have been tried, but with only partial success; but all concur in the opinion that the eggs of diseased subjects are unfit for use, and should be rejected.

It has been demonstrated also that the grubs, the chrysalides, and the moths proceeding from the Japanese race or that of the South American states, have been to the present moment free from all trace of corpuscules and all symptoms of the disease.

Practical breeders of the south of France have made very interesting experiments, from which it resulted that the worm when hatched and bred in stables or in sheep folds generally did well.

Comparative experiments prove that the same lot of eggs divided into two parts gave products good in quality and quantity as to the half raised in the atmosphere of a stable, while the grubs of the other part bred under the ordinary conditions generally perished.

These repeated trials appear to demonstrate that the grave nature of the affliction can be modified by the alkalinity of the atmosphere which developes itself in so declared a manner under the conditions of which we have just spoken. It is a species of treatment analogous to that of the water and salt of Vichy and other thermal springs.

BREEDING OF SILK-WORMS.

The industry whose object is the production of cocoons is composed of elements so special and so different from those of manufactures in general as to require that some details be given on the subject, partly agricultural and partly manufacturing.

The basis of the labor of the silk-worm breeder is founded in general on the amount of mulberry leaves consumed. These leaves constitute in this case the raw material.

We will give some figures derived from localities where the population is relatively condensed, such as the south of France and the north of

Italy, the principal European centres for rearing the silk-worm and the mulberry.

A hectare (or $2\frac{471}{1000}$ acres) of land, planted with 2,500 mulberry trees, produces annually an average of 5,000 kilograms of leaves. The expenses of all kinds for the culture of this quantity may amount to 350 francs a year. Then the 1,000 kilograms of leaves amount to 70 francs. The 1,000 kilograms of leaves support a variable quantity of cocoons. In normal years it may amount to 60 kilograms.

Taking the 1,000 kilograms of leaves as the unit, the average expenses for feeding worms for 30 grams of eggs are as follows:

	Francs.	
30 grams of eggs, with a price very variable, are at the maximum	15	= $3
1,000 kilograms of leaves	70	= 14
Manual labor of two persons during 40 days	160	= 32
Warming and lighting	10	= 2
Cells for cocoons, and incidental expenses	5	= 1
Total	260	= 52

The fresh cocoons are now worth at least eight francs the kilogram. It would be sufficient to obtain 32 kilograms for every 1,000 kilograms of leaves to pay the disbursements, and if the gatherings yield, as is usual in normal conditions, 50 kilograms only, this would be a gain of 50 times eight, or 400 francs, ($80,) and if one worked on a basis of one hectare of land only, this would be a gain of 400 times five, or 2,000 francs ($400) in six weeks. There were breeders in France who, before the epidemic, produced as many as 1,000 kilograms of cocoons in a single season.

APPARATUS USED IN THE MANUFACTURE OF SILK.

TOOLS OR STOCK NECESSARY TO TRANSFORM THE COCOONS INTO RAW SILK.

France and Italy are the only countries which have exhibited the apparatus necessary to transform the cocoons into threads of silk. These are the most advanced in the whole of Europe in this specialty.

The industry of Spain, of Greece, of the Levant, and of Russia, has imitated as much as possible the means used in France and Italy. Those countries have not, however, been able to arrive at the perfection of their neighbors. As to the Orientals, they lose a part of the advantages which their privileged climate gives them in regard to the production of silk by insufficiency of care and skill in details.

The implements, properly so-called, for converting the cocoons, are most simple in all countries of the world. They consist principally of a basin and a reel. The basin is used to receive the cocoons and some warm water to soften the gum of the silken envelope, so as to set free the threads forming the exterior silky layers. The union of a certain number of these threads forms the thread of commerce known by the name of *grège*, or raw silk.

The reel, by its rotary motion, winds off the cocoons. In the factories, certain numbers of these winding machines are placed side by side, the impulsion being given to them by a single motive power. Of course the arrangement is such that the operator can, at will, stop any of these little contrivances while the others continue to work. The entirety of the operation is automatic, except that in regard to each reel we find a basin and a woman to superintend the work. The labors of the superintendent consist—

1. In the immersion of the cocoons in the warm water until the silky layers are sufficiently softened.

2. In the cleansing, with a species of brush or broom, of the first layers until they become a pure and clean thread.

3. In the uniting by pressure and twisting a certain number of threads of the cocoons in proportion to the standard of raw silk intended to be produced.

The *grège* thus formed by the union of a greater or less number of cocoons is passed through an orifice or drawing frame, which acts on the winder, whose rotation determines the development of the threads of the cocoons which remain immersed on the surface of the water in the basin, so that in proportion as the cocoons are wound off, the attendant is careful to add a new one, as much to keep up the supply of thread as to maintain the regularity of the standard.

The cocoons being conical from the commencement to the end of the winding, the *grège* would have the greatest irregularities if the workman did not conduct his work so as to connect the strongest, that is to say the commencement of the thread of the new cocoon, with those which are just being exhausted.

The threads, issuing wet and gummy from the basin, would adhere and stick together in the skein if careful means were not taken to prevent it. The preventive consists first in preserving a sufficient distance between the basin and the reel, to permit a partial drying; and second in a " guide thread" so arranged that the transport takes place by a slow zigzag movement, which prevents the threads from crossing each other at the same point at each turn, which latter causes the adhesion.

Some suggestions will assist us to understand and to obviate the difficulties in this branch of the work.

The degree of previous preparation should vary with the durability of the silky couches, having regard to the age, breed, and origin of the cocoons.

If prepared too much, the result would be that more silky matter would be yielded by the first layers than there should be. This superfluous matter would be only waste, and would possess a value much inferior to that of fine silk.

If the cocoons are, on the contrary, insufficiently prepared, they present a resistance to the winding off, which causes the breaking of the thread, and leads to a new source of waste. The workman ought to possess great skill in joining a new thread to a thread in work. He should be competent to select the most opportune moment to assure the regularity of the product, so that the trace of these successive connections may be imperceptible to the eye, and thus avoid knots, coarseness, curls, or dots.

Nor will rare skill in these particulars produce the effect desired, unless the wheel revolves with a fixed and steady velocity of at least 500 metres per minute. Without this, the thread, instead of being smooth and brilliant, would be rough and dull.

A too slow movement would not dress the thread sufficiently, clasped, as it is, very tightly by its peculiar position and fixed under the form of the figure 8 in the layers of the cocoons. A movement too slow causes those undulations which give the dull appearance; while the development of the thread in the straight line by the more rapid movement permits the reflection of the light in those perfect and determined conditions which give brilliancy to the finest silk.

We have entered somewhat at length into these details because they will assist us to discover the many difficult sides of a question of apparent simplicity, and will enable us the better to understand why the more perfect development of this industry remains concentrated in the hands of some populations, and why automatic labor has not been able, till now, to bring about those elaborate and exquisite modifications in silk which have been produced in other textile fabrics. But if converting the cocoons into raw silk in a successful manner be due to local circumstances, such is not the case with the industrial specialties which follow it, commencing with the throwing or spinning of the silk.

Almost all European nations were represented at the Exposition by the different mechanisms employed in the silk manufacture. Let us take a glance at the machines of this character. We will first speak of the machinery used to sort and dress silk badly reeled, and it may be well to enter into some details on this subject, as it is one that particularly interests the American manufacturers.

Silk of the first quality being actually as dear as silver,[1] ought to be employed only in the best and most perfect conditions, especially when it is intended to produce fabrics like those so much admired at the Exposition, and among others the truly artistic silks of Lyons. Different means have been devised to determine the standard of the silk thread. If it be pure it will have the degree of solidity and tenacity desired. The manufacturer is particularly ingenious in constructing apparatus to rectify, sort, and dress silks of irregular standards.

---

[1] In spite of the high price and the crisis in silk husbandry, silk costs much less than in the time of the Romans. The Emperor Aurelian refused a silk dress to his wife, assigning as a reason that it was too expensive a luxury even for a Roman empress, silk then being sold for its weight in gold, pound for pound.

APPARATUS TO SORT, TO PROVE, AND TEST THE QUALITIES AND PROP-
ERTIES OF SILK.

Silk thread has more need to be sorted or numbered than the thread of other substances; the sorting or numbering is to determine the relation of the unity of weight to the unity of length. For silk the unity of weight is generally the *denier* or fraction of the ancient *livre* of Montpellier, and the *denier* is equivalent to 0.53 of the *livre*.

The unit of length is 400 *aunes*, representing 475 metres, or 515 yards. Thus, when we say a silk of $\frac{8}{9}$ *deniers*, we mean that a thread of it of 475 metres of length weighs from eight to nine *deniers*.[1]

Efforts are being made to modify this standard and to substitute the unit of 500 metres for the 475 metres, and the milligram for the *denier*, in order to make the system conform to the metrical system.

The rectification of the standard of silk seems to be more necessary than that of other valuable materials, because, from the manner silk is produced, we are far less sure to arrive at regularity than by the automatic process practiced for the conversion of cotton, wool, &c.

Besides, as silk, from its nature and price, is intended for the dearest kind of products, the material employed in its manufacture ought to be so much the more perfect. The mode of *titrage* generally used in all periods consists in winding off a certain length, and the determination of the weight of this length. The less it weighs, the finer, of course, the silk will be.

It is considered, for example, that if 500 metres weigh one milligram, it will be one-half more fine than if it weighed two milligrams, supposing always that its hygrometric and thermometric condition does not change during the operations. The same unit of length will weigh more if it contains humidity than if it be perfectly dry.

The public establishments of Europe to ascertain the condition of silk have for their specific object to determine, in an exact manner, the real state of the silk, its degree of humidity, and the absolute weight of this same foreign matter, as if the silk were perfectly dry.

Establishments of this kind, it is well known, exist in the principal manufacturing centres of the trade in silk and wool. They generally operate under the direction of the various chambers of commerce.

These means of control offer a great security to business, but unhappily they can do nothing to verify or establish the regularity of the threads.

The *titrage* gives, in effect, only the relation between the weight and the length, but indicates nothing as to the homogeneity of the thread. Each determinate length of a skein may have identical weight without the thread being regular. For example, if a skein of 10,000 metres presents an equal *titre* or standard for each 1,000 metres, that would not demonstrate that upon this length there may not be parts alternately

---

[1] Condition publique des soies et des laines, bureau de titrage. Décret du 2 Mai, 1853.

coarse and fine. This effect happens much more frequently with the silks that are poorly worked, on account of their low relative price.

Some sellers in China, Japan, and the Levant, strive, with great persistency, to ascertain and rectify these irregularities of thread by the windings off. During this process, when the eye discovers the defects, they are removed by the hand; but this is a slow, expensive operation, and anything but sure.

The Swiss exhibition contained an automatic apparatus which arrives much more efficiently and economically at the result sought for.

THE SILK-SORTING APPARATUS OF G. HONNEGER, SWITZERLAND.

This machine receives on the one part a series of skeins of silk. To each skein correspond a number of bobbins or reels, equal to that of the varied bulk supposed to be contained in the skein.

The solution of the problem consists in collecting on each bobbin thread of the same fineness. Let us suppose five bobbins from No. 1 to No. 5. Each will receive the portion of the thread of the *titre* for which it shall have been designated. For this purpose the thread which is rendered from the skein to the bobbins is guided automatically by a mechanism for gauging, extremely sensitive, and so arranged that the *grège* or raw silk in passing acts upon a lever which directs the silk upon the proper bobbin.

The variation in the bulk of the product is the point of departure in the variation of the guide lever, which directs the thread to the reel proper to receive it.

A glance at the working of this apparatus enables us to understand it better than would the most elaborate description.

By the employment of this machine the cheap silk of the east can hereafter find still more extensive applications, and contribute to a new development in silk industry.

AN APPARATUS TO TRY THREADS BY PROFESSOR ALCAN.

Another apparatus of great utility was exhibited by Professor Alcan in the French section. It is an instrument of rare precision, very simple, not expensive, and works with great facility. Its object is to test the tenacity and elasticity of filaments and threads, and to determine the degree of tension most suitable to be employed on any given thread.

The mechanism of this instrument, though not at all complicated, has been explained in detail, with its applications, by the inventor, in several works very popular in France, particularly in his treatise upon the textile arts, one of which is entitled "On Cotton Labor," and the other "On the Manufacture of Wool."

These works of M. Michel Alcan, Professor of the *Conservatoire Impérial des Arts et Métiers de Paris* are to be obtained by the publisher, J. Baudry, Paris.

We name these works because they give a greater amount of information upon the production of raw material and upon the progress of this industry than any other works within our knowledge.

Near this machine at the Exposition is another apparatus called *Expérimentateur Phrosodynamique*, to prove threads; and also a new machine to prepare and open cotton before the ginning, both the production of Professor Alcan. This eminent engineer has made, as we have seen, a special study of the industrial questions which are of such vast importance to the American people.

IMPLEMENTS AND APPARATUS USED IN SILK-THROWING.

The machines for "silk-throwing" seen at the Exposition have remained, as far as fundamental principles are concerned, in the same general condition wherein they were at the origin of automatic industry; but they have been improved in their details, and in the harmony of their execution.

The Swiss manufacturers, especially, have exhibited a remarkable collection of implements in this department.

The assortment as thus exposed, and which is employed in the best factories, consists—

1. Of series of *tarelles* to wind, clean, and equalize the threads during their automatic winding off.

2. Of an apparatus to unite and double the threads with a mechanism for instantly stopping the machine whenever a thread breaks.

3. Of a machine to give the first twist to the double threads in the direction determined for the production of the tram or woof.

4. Of a second machine to retwist together two threads already twisted separately, thus producing the organzine.

The object of these machines, so simple in their construction, is to obtain constantly an evenly twisted product—that is to say, worked in such a manner that each unit of length receives exactly the same number of turns.

Now the realization of this object was not effected without encountering difficulties which have been completely surmounted by the Swiss and French mechanicians, judging as well from the machines as from the magnificent threads exhibited.

This class of machinery is the more advanced because the machines to convert silk are, of all others, the cheapest, and this results directly from their greater simplification.

The "throwing" the threads of silk has several objects in view.

1. It gives them a sufficient resistance to admit of their being boiled in soapy water to remove the gummy matter, so that they may receive the dye better and give greater brilliancy than if they had remained in the raw state.

2. By the ungumming the silk acquires the desired suppleness of silks called "boiled," whilst if it retained its gum it would be stiff and rough, like the silks employed in bareges, for example.

3. The throwing the silk is intended to give a certain peculiar appearance to the threads, which partly determines what is called the grain of the stuff.

Moreover, when these threads are intended for brilliant tissues, such as satins, the two successive torsions which constitute the organzine are combined in such a manner that the last, which will be the most apparent, should have the least twist in order to preserve the brilliancy of the stuff.

The combination is inverted if the object be to make threads for taffetas, gros grain, gros de Naples, &c.

The work of silk-throwing, by the combination of the varied conditions it requires, necessitates the possession of such accurate knowledge, and the use of such rare skill as to constitute it a special art.

SIMULTANEOUS REELING AND THROWING.

It has been frequently attempted, and is sometimes still sought, to unite in one single operation the winding off of the cocoons and the throwing of the silk. Notwithstanding that for a long time the solution of this problem, which apparently presents no serious difficulty, has been considered as the philosopher's stone of silk industry, the effort has not been abandoned. Still in this department, as certain mechanism exhibited by the Italians and French attest, the problem offers but little interest or encouragement; as for example, to wind off the cocoons and twist the thread at the same time, the raw silk or *grège* in issuing from the basins, instead of being passed on to the reels by one simple movement, is rolled around bobbins having a rotary motion, in order to give torsion to the threads.

It is necessary to direct two of them together upon one bobbin to produce the tram; consequently the intermediate operations are all suppressed and condensed into one single process, and hence an apparent economy; but, in fact, this economy disappears and the new mode becomes comparatively expensive, because the production is considerably reduced and because it requires a much larger personal attendance.

A few figures will suffice to demonstrate this. To produce the *grège*, the velocity most suitable is such that one workman throws out at least a length of 500 metres of thread a minute.

When the thread is twisted at the same time only 500 revolutions are given per metre to it in the majority of cases. Suppose a velocity of 3,000 revolutions to the spindles, only six metres will be produced instead of 500 a minute. It is true a workwoman can superintend four threads instead of one, but it will still be necessary to employ twenty times as many spinners in this case as when the production of the *grège* was in question.

Now this augmentation of expense is much more considerable than the economy realized by the suppression of the intermediate operations. But the most serious difficulty consists in the imperfection of the results.

The slowness of motion in the simultaneous twisting and throwing does not permit a suitable development to be given to the thread, nor a sufficient tension for the entire unwinding which causes the dark aspect of the product already spoken of.

In a word, by the combination of different operations, the workman is not able to bestow upon his task that care in cleansing and purifying which is performed by the automatic system and by hand as it exists in careful silk-throwing.

Thus the apparent progress, so enticing in appearance, demands an expense much more considerable than that of the separate operations mentioned, and can only give inferior products of inconsiderable value.

In order that they may be forewarned, these facts are worthy of special notice by the American people, who are only beginning to turn their attention to this branch of industry.

However, all new attempts may reach ultimate success; and if it be true that for beautiful normal products the simultaneous twisting and throwing must be rejected, there are cases where they may be employed, and, indeed, where they begin to be employed with a certain success; as for example, when the cocoons are of an inferior quality, and difficult to wind off, such as double cocoons, so that the operator in twisting them directly can, at the best, obtain silk of only a very inferior grade, fit only for working common *cordonnet*, (braid, binding, twist, lace, &c.) In such case the simultaneous process may be advantageously used. And, indeed, cocoons, wound and doubled and twisted simultaneously, in order to make directly from them certain products intended for *passementeries* or trimmings, have no need of such careful superintendence as would be required in regard to the same cocoons when intended to produce the more beautiful silks. A single person can attend a greater number of ends, (or *bouts*,) inasmuch as these coarse articles are far less liable to break.

There are then two conditions which permit the employment of the simultaneous system with advantage.

1. When the object to be attained is not an imperfect *grège*, but a *cordonnet* for trimmings, of a sufficiently good quality, and at a price relatively high; and 2d, in cases where the expense of hand labor is considerably reduced in consequence of the character and destiny of the special product—one person under such circumstances being able to produce very much more than he otherwise would by the ordinary process.

PRODUCTION AND UTILITY OF SILK WASTE.

The different transformations undergone by silk, up to this point, and those it has still to undergo until it arrives at the state of "stuff," occasions "waste."

This waste presents itself in different states. Those resulting from the operations which precede the torsion offer parcels of raw filaments (*grège*) not twisted, known by the name of *frisons*, or waste from reeling cocoons.

There are *frisons* of different qualities, according to the period of preparation given to them, or according as they proceed from *cocons dégrainés* or *percés*. In this case the waste is more particularly designated by the name *golette*, from which are made coarse silks called *fantaisie*, *chappe*, &c.

The waste proceeding from the different manipulations, commencing with the winding off of the *grège*, in the throwing, and the operations of weaving, is generally composed of twisted ends, and is known by the name of *bourre*.

These two sorts of *débris* have been long utilized. They are divided, cleansed, ungummed, and then equalized by cutting to prepare them for twisting, as we have already said. But there is another kind of waste, long neglected, and which has commenced to be utilized only since the very high price of silk, namely, the *chiffons*, or rags of this material. Establishments of this kind are very rare; one exists in England, one in France, and a third in the United States. We have no knowledge of any other.

As to the winding of waste, we must limit ourselves to pointing out a certain progress, of which threads of this kind have been the subject as well in France as in Switzerland.

NEW THREADS OF SILK BOURRE.

We have seen, in the show cases of the Exhibition of these two countries, threads from *bourre*, (a sort of shoddy,) which rival in the beauty of their appearance the most lustrous silks, and at one-half the price.

These results are obtained by attention to details in the manufacture. All these operations have attained remarkable precision, and have been executed conformably to the indications of science, and by the application of certain preparations under special conditions. When the threads have been produced with the greatest care from waste, well purified, well combed, perfectly prepared and spun, the workman then proceeds to apply a thin layer or coating of warm gelatine or isinglass to the thread when stretched and in motion.

The drying and ulterior *chevillage* completes the work, and imparts to the products that peculiar brilliancy so much esteemed, and that elasticity so indispensable to manufactures of this kind.

The unusual care and attention brought to the working up of waste have been necessitated, as we have said, by the rise in the price of this material. It is not many years since the waste, which at present sells at from 12 to 15 francs, was worth only four or five francs, the kilogram.

This fact alone is sufficient to justify the efforts made to utilize waste of every description.

Formerly certain sweepings of threads were thrown on the waste heap which the workmen knew not how to unravel; but for the disintegration of these the most ingenious and effective machines have been devised.

These machines take the rag or piece of silk at its entrance, restore it at its exit in the form of filaments, carefully classed in lengths and fineness, proper to be submitted to the machines for decomposing the *chiffon* or rag.

The inventors have not exhibited these machines, from fear of imitation by countries where inventions are not protected by patents. Prussia and Switzerland are in this condition, and they are precisely the countries which would derive the greatest advantage from their use.

DYEING AND SURCHARGE OF THREADS.

We have but little to say on the dyeing of silk, so brilliant in itself, and advanced to such an extraordinary degree of perfection.

No kind of material offers more splendor in this respect.

The invention of those colors derived from coal has principally contributed to or caused this revolution in the art of dyeing. The new materials have permitted dyers to obtain colors of unprecedented splendor, combining shades of marvellous variety with extreme delicacy. Looking through the Exhibition we might almost say, in the presence of the results obtained in this direction, there is now nothing impossible. Still, close by the side of products so admirable in respect to dyeing, we saw, on the contrary, much still left to be accomplished. We refer to the attempts made for some time to gild and silver threads of silk. Some specimens of silk of this kind exhibited denote processes still in a crude state, which do not yet supply any product capable of being used advantageously.

Another branch of dyeing is, on the contrary, in a very advanced state; sometimes too advanced.

Reference is here made to the means used to *surcharge* silks, so as to make them gain, if one wished it, as much as one hundred per cent. upon their normal weight.

This process has an honest origin, and sometimes its applications are honest; but it is not unfrequently used for purposes of gross deception. For example, when the threads and tissues are sold by length or by surface, these surcharges have no other result than to give a certain appearance to the article, while the thickness of the tissue plays no other part here than that which frequently results from the stiffness of stuffs of this sort, without any detriment to the buyer. But, on the other hand, when the threads and even the tissues are sold by weight, it makes the purchaser pay the price of silk for a considerable quantity of foreign matter which, sometimes, has not a fortieth part of the value of silk.

Nevertheless the authors of these operations, whose main object is to give increased weight to silk, are tolerated and even rewarded at the Exhibition, under the pretext that they thereby aid in meeting foreign competition.

These are specious pretexts which ought to be made known. As these efforts for facilitating the best employment of waste are worthy to be pointed out and recommended, so, on the contrary, these reprehensible practices are to be deplored and condemned.

WEAVING.

THE WEAVING OF STUFFS OF ONE COLOR, VELVETY, OR PILED FABRICS.

We observed at the Exhibition some plain silks made in France, Switzerland, and northern Germany, leaving nothing in this department to desire.

This result proves, that if the automatic working of plain silk goods be not yet general, it results from special causes in the organization of the fabrics, rather than from difficulties in the execution of the work, for the perfect specimens hereinbefore mentioned were exhibited with the special notice that the weaving was done by motive power.

We examined with care the looms by which this result has been attained. Looms of this kind were exhibited in the English, French, and Swiss sections of the Exposition. The two latter nations have more especially applied themselves to the construction of looms intended for silk weaving, while the English looms, being adapted to more general use in the weaving of almost every kind of fabrics, are not so well fitted to the weaving of silk, which demands particular care and special adaptation.

The Swiss and French also make the *canettes* for the tram, the *ourdissoirs*, destined to dispose the *chaine*, and the arrangements for raising and advancing it on the loom.

They thus have an appearance peculiarly their own. Competent men quickly observe that certain alterations, which influence only the proportions and relations between the different means generally used in all looms of this kind, and, in this case, important modifications.

These changes are especially employed in utilizing the peculiar elasticity of silk, so as to obtain from it the regularity which the interlacing of threads in silk goods demands, and also to be better able to secure cleanness, purity, and brilliancy.

By the side of the machines and apparatus of which we have just spoken was exhibited a French machine, to polish automatically these same stuffs. This machine, alike ingenious and efficacious, possesses all the advantages of hand polishing, acting with only a little polish and in parts.

All these machines have great value and interest for American industry; and it is the same with the automatic looms for the manufacture of velvet stuffs, such as plush for hats, &c.

These automatic looms may be arranged in two classes. The one class works two pieces at one time; the other only one. Both have their special object and employment.

The loom which makes two pieces at the same time is furnished with three chains superposed, the one above the other, at suitable distances. The middle chain is intended to supply the thread which, by the *coupé* or cutting, forms the velvet surface. The middle chain, or *chaîne de poil*, has a much greater length than that of the other two. It is proportional to the length of the piece multiplied by the height of the *doret*, and by the number of *boucles* or loops necessary to each of them.

The interlacings in the weaving of these three *chaînes* are such that they form two *toiles* or fabrics, between which is interlaced a certain height of the thread of the *chaine*. This height is exactly and automatically separated in two by the middle one, in order to supply the velvet surface to each piece, which, thus separated, is then rolled upon a roller as fast as the section is worked.

Various articles in silk, and especially the most beautiful plushes for hats, are executed in this manner.

This system is more particularly suited to plain articles wherein the *doret*, without the intervention of the *baguettes* or small rings employed in hand-weaving, necessitates a certain height, and can be employed to manufacture *façonnées* or figured stuffs and very smooth velvets.

The automatic work in smooth and fine velvets has yet only reached the extent of weaving one piece at a time. The operation is effected by the insertion of irons to determine the *boucles* or loops which remain closed in the work of velvet *frisé*. The iron is withdrawn when a certain number of *boucles* or loops are fixed by interlacements.

If, on the contrary, the object is to make velvet *coupé*, it is effected by cutting at the top each of these loops or *boucles*.

Thus, to the ordinary functions of weaving machines, it is necessary in the weaving of velvets to add combinations, which place and withdraw *baguettes* to form the *frisure* in which these *baguettes* are placed, and act as a knife or plane to cut these same loops in order to produce cut velvet.

These problems have been solved in the most successful manner by the looms at the Exposition. It need hardly be suggested that a personal examination of the machines above mentioned would give a far clearer idea of their structure and mode of operation than could the most elaborate description. The same may be said of the machines hereinafter noticed.

If from plain articles we pass to striped and plaid silks, in the execution of which Scotch industry has long excelled, we shall encounter some difficulty and embarrassment in choosing from among the numerous automatic looms now multiplied to a marvellous extent, permitting the frame to change spontaneously a greater or less number of trams of different colors. The numerous looms of this kind exhibited demonstrate the activity and necessity of research in this direction, and also the energy with which science and skill are employed on all those problems whose solution can lead to utility and economy.

It is not only in articles of an ordinary character that this tendency is observable. It is no less remarkable in silks of the richest devices, and especially in the most beautiful articles of Lyons adapted as well for dresses as for furniture.

THE WEAVING OF FAÇONNÉS.

It is worthy of note that despite the increasing dearness of silk thread these silks, so very rich in all the perfection of their manufacture, are not sensibly increased in price.

Never perhaps have the stuffs of Lyons displayed more taste than now. Never have they or those of Tours exhibited greater beauty and perfection.

Among the silks for toilette we remark, especially in the *façonnés* or figured goods, a fineness and neatness that seemed almost impossible till now, which denote a superiority to which French industry alone has yet arrived.

There are also combination *armures* and *moirés* as the basis of tissues, demonstrating that there no longer exist difficulties in this direction.

It was sufficient to traverse the gallery of the French machines to be fully impressed with these views. Ingenuity has been tasked in a thousand different ways to simplify the elements of the Jacquard loom and render it capable of producing still more extensive results.

It secures economy in the use of the cards, necessitated by this manufacture, by diminishing the surface of holes, or *trous*, and of the folds which separate them, in such a manner as to make them contain more in a given surface.

Besides the cards entirely dispensed with and replaced by a simple sheet of paper, further on, there is an ingenious combination which premits the same card to serve twice successively and to produce two different effects, and enables it also to economize at least 50 per cent. of cards.

There are savings of another kind in the automatic execution of stitching, due to the introduction of an additional organ into the frame to make *façonnés le battant brocheur.*

Blonde, an article in silk imitating lace, is also exhibited by both England and France. This article, made automatically, and which for years has displayed the most elegant designs, now presents devices the most capricious and seducing. These results are attained by the combination of the net lace frame with the principle of the Jacquard frame, skilfully modified in its applications.

Until now, manufacturers were content to vary the designs and multiply the figures, and hence a single loom of this kind produced with considerable economy hundreds of *bandes* at once. But that was not sufficient. The industry of Calais (the centre of the *tulle* and *blonde* trade of France) had just created an article essentially different from ordinary lace and *blonde.* It was obtained by the interlacement of threads acting exclusively in the direction of the *chaine* in the *tissues à maille,* to which we have alluded.

A transversal thread of the tram made a part of the tissue, the physiognomy of which and the mode of interlacing being thus essentially modified. The modifications, proceeding from an additional cross-thread, could be carried upon the *réseaux* from the bottom, and those of the *façonnée* at the same time.

A new and vast field thus opens to the specialty of reticular tissues, already so rich in fancy articles. Perhaps also this kind of stuff will pass from silk to cotton, and to other substances, and ultimately give results analogous to those of a species of ganze, which is produced, if not with great difficulty, at least with great slowness, and at considerable cost.

The new article may probably serve as tissues for sifting flour and all kinds of plaster substances.

The mechanical means by which these results are attained, and many others into the details of which we cannot now enter, combining with the use in a greater and constantly increasing extent of cheap silks, demonstrate a gratifying progress in this direction.

SILK RIBBONS.

We have only spoken briefly of ribbons from a technical point of view, because this industry was represented at the Exposition by but one loom, that for velvet, sent by M. Joyot, jr..

As to the products, they were exhibited for the most part collectively by the manufacturers of Saint Etienne, Basle, Prussia, Alsace, and other sections.

Saint Etienne contains 90,000 inhabitants, and with its suburbs gives employment to 23,622 persons, of which the greater part are women and girls. It has 15,000 looms. According to the Chamber of Commerce, the value of its productions for the year 1866 was 60,000,000 francs, ($12,000,000,) five-sixths of which was disposed of to the United States, England, and to the city of Paris.

The canton of Basle, with a population of 65,000 inhabitants, has about 6,000 looms for the manufacture of ribbons in the city of Basle alone. The manufacturers, many of whom are of the first order, employ from 300 to 400 hands each, while some few employ a much larger number. The United States takes the largest quantity of these goods. Then comes England, whose trade in continental silks has greatly augmented since the last treaty of commerce with France. It was at Guebwiller, in Alsace, that steam was first employed in the manufacture of ribbons. One may see there a mode ribbon factory which employs 600 persons, and contains 200 looms driven by a steam engine of 30-horse power.

DEPENDENCE OF SILK MANUFACTURERS UPON THE EAST.

In view of the vast capital invested in silk industry, and especially in silk manufactures, by leading European nations, and the great number of their people employed in its prosecution, we may, in the presence of the crisis which has overtaken their silk husbandmen on account of the prevailing malady, pertinently ask what would have been the fate of the industry and the condition of its employés had not the extreme east been able to supply them with raw material in quantities sufficient to meet the exigency? And what advantages have not the nations of Asia derived from being thus brought into closer relations with the more elevated and advanced nations of western Europe? Notwithstanding the relatively low price at which they can supply their silks, they could not, a quarter of a century since, have anticipated so high a price as they are now receiving. Nor is this the only advantage resulting to these oriental nations from this species of traffic with the silk manufacturers of Europe. It will teach them how to bring their products to greater perfection at home, and will stimulate them to prepare them with such care, and bestow upon them such an amount of skilled labor, as to draw from them all the value and profit that comports with the excellence of their nature.

RÉSUMÉ AND CONCLUSION.

The manufacture of silk as already analyzed, and as it exists in countries the most advanced in the art, embraces seven special branches of industry, viz:

1. The rearing of the silk-worms.
2. The filature or reeling of the silk from the cocoons.
3. The throwing or spinning of the silk thread.
4. The dyeing of the silk.
5. The preparation of the silk threads for the looms.
6. The weaving of silk goods.
7. The spinning of waste silk.

These specialties, although consequent and dependent each upon the others like links in a chain, can nevertheless be practiced separately, as is the case now in some countries.

We have demonstrated that some of these employments present more difficulties than others to countries which, like the United States, have not yet had sufficient experience therein. America can, however, hope henceforth to excel in these industries whenever she resolutely wills it, and devotes to them that energy and skill which have placed her in the first rank among nations for certain of her inventions and manufactures. Let her not be disheartened at her efforts in this branch of industry, already most praiseworthy, and especially so in New Jersey, Connecticut, New York and Massachusetts, Pennsylvania and California; but let her press on and bring to this new enterprise that genius of investigation and energy in execution which have attracted to her so much attention, and attained for her such honorable distinction in the Universal Exhibition of 1867.

Concerning the seven industrial branches employed in the transformations of silk, four can from this period develop themselves without any difficulty, and soon take, in America, the high position already attained by cotton industry, namely:

1. The throwing of the silk, consisting in the employment of apparatus more simple and also less difficult to direct than the greater part of the machines in the factories of the United States. As to the raw material, it is as easy for the United States as for England to immediately supply herself with raw silk in China, Japan, and even in the Levant and India. It is by no means improbable that at no distant day New York will become as important a depot of Asiatic silks as London now is. This may be accomplished via San Francisco through the medium of the Pacific railway. The raw material having thus reached New York, will be distributed not only among our own manufacturers, but portions doubtless will be exported to foreign countries. Let the New World take England as an example in silk industry. In less than half a century the silk manufacture of Great Britain (which does not produce a single pound of silk upon her own soil) has arrived at such a degree of development as to give employment to a large amount of capital and to about 110,000 looms, and direct occupation to some 200,000 persons, not including those engaged in the ribbon and silk hosiery manufacture.

2. The dyeing of silk, already an established branch of American industry, needs only the encouragement to be derived from the establishment of co-operative branches to compete successfully with European skill.

The preparatory processes of ungumming, cleansing, and scouring, are very simple operations, and can be entered upon without delay.

3. As to the regeneration and spinning of silky waste of all kinds, the United States find themselves in as good a position as most other countries to undertake a work of this sort, inasmuch as they possess equal facilities for procuring the waste and raw silk.

Who can doubt, therefore, that this will soon become an important branch of American industry?

In the manufacture of *passementerie* or trimmings, made to a great extent of silk waste, there are employed in Paris alone 8,500 persons, producing annually products to the value of about $8,000,000.

This branch of industry throughout France occupies more than 30,000 hands, and the entire annual production exceeds $20,000,000. It is one of the occupations which, like the manufacture of ribbons and laces, employs the largest number of women and children, who earn from 20 to 60 cents per day.

The wages depend both upon the skill of the laborer and the nature of the work. Men earn from 60 cents to $1 50 per day.

St. Etienne is noted for its fashionable dress trimmings; St. Chamond for its excellent cords, braids, and stay-laces, employing about 2,000 frames, or *métiers à la poupée*, in weaving stay-laces alone.

Most of these articles are extensively copied by foreign manufacturers from samples obtained in Paris. A system has been inaugurated there for promptly supplying samples of all novelties in silk fabrics by the payment of a yearly subscription.

4. With regard to the automatic weaving of plain stuffs, the United States already compete successfully with the more experienced nations of Europe. It is gratifying to know that the looms exhibited by American constructors have been highly appreciated for their ingenious contrivances and remarkable improvements.[1]

There remain, then, three specialties, to excel in which time will be necessary to obtain the experience requisite for complete success. This our countrymen will indubitably acquire in due season, if they will only bring to the task their usual sagacity and proverbial perseverance.

These specialties are:

1. The rearing of silk-worms.
2. The reeling of the cocoons into raw silk.
3. The weaving of figured goods more or less rich.

We will speak of them in their order:

First. As to rearing of the silk-worm. The most important element in this matter seems to be solved, namely: the culture of the mulberry. The various previous trials in the United States already mentioned have proved that large sections of the country are admirably suited to the growth of this tree, so indispensable to the rearing of the worm. And from what has already been shown it may be inferred that if the breeding of silk-worms has not been hitherto entirely successful, it is probably because that, at the periods of these early attempts, the agricultural population was not sufficiently instructed in details, and therefore failed in some essential particulars, or lacked somewhat of that patience which the French and Italian cultivators bring to this particular pursuit. But with an increase of experience, daily augmented by recruits to our population from the skilled labor of Europe and China, with individualities and talents the most diverse and elastic, with abundance of capital seeking investment, and above all, with our fertile and remunerative soils, and the superior climatic conditions of large sections of our country, it is not possible that new trials, judiciously conducted, should fail of success.[2]

---

[1] The looms exhibited by Mr. M. Opper, of New York, Mr. George Crompton, of Worcester, Massachusetts, and the knitting machine of Mr. J. W. Lamb, of Rochester, attracted special attention, and a silver medal was awarded for each.

[2] As a proof how the introduction of this industry into a locality will enhance the prosperity of a whole people, an interesting fact may be cited from a recent French publication. An officer in the French army, having seen during an Italian campaign to what degree the cultivation of the mulberry tree and its attendant silk husbandry were enriching the population, resolved to introduce it into the little vale in the commune of Vallerangue, where he owned an estate. Soon after the introduction there was obtained there only some 2,000 kilograms, of very poor unsalable cocoons. But, after a few years, 200,000 kilograms, of an excellent quality, were produced annually, valued at 1,000,000 of francs, (say $200,000,) which sum was mostly diffused among the rural laboring population of a village of 4,000 inhabitants. The work was carried on in the following manner: the well-to-do proprietors

Second. The reeling or filature of the cocoons into raw silk, which comes next in order, constitutes, perhaps, one of the processes the most difficult **to** teach, **and** especially in localities wanting in experience in this particular branch **of** silk industry.

The superiority of the French and Italian silks over Asiatic **silks is** generally owing to the perfection of reeling. The success of this process depends, in a large measure, upon the care and watchfulness of the attendant, especially so far as the perfection of the product is concerned.

The rapid analysis above made of this kind of labor may assist us to understand the difficulty that besets this branch of the work; but we shall render it still more palpable by saying that the most experienced workwomen can hardly produce more than 300 grams (or 12 ounces) in good silk of the ordinary qualities obtained from five or six cocoons per thread, of which the quality or fineness is from 10 to 12 *denier*, being 24,000 yards **per** ounce.

Nevertheless, the country which produces the most skilful and careful spinners of **wool and cotton** manufactures will not despair of arriving eventually at the successful production of the many kinds of silk goods so clearly within its province.

Third. Though we feel assured that the industry of the United States will soon largely develop itself in the weaving of plain, striped, and plaid silks, **of** velvets, of plain ribbons, and other silk fabrics, simple in their character, yet we cannot conceal the fact that long and patient study is necessary to produce articles of sufficient novelty and artistic skill to compete with European industry, and more particularly with that of Lyons, which shines with a brilliancy peculiarly its own.

The great experience, cultivated taste, and extensive knowledge **of the** French, have made this specialty with them a veritable art.

The employment of Jacquard looms forms the basis of success in textile fabrics. But although this loom is universally in use, the effects it can produce have been nowhere pushed to so great an extent as in France, and particularly in Lyons.

The same may be said of Calais in its application of the Jacquard to *blondes*, or figured silk laces.

The Exposition proves, by products of this kind, that henceforth to automatic labor almost nothing is impossible.

The magnificent specimens of lace there displayed, which imitate and well nigh rival the most exquisite and elaborate efforts obtained by the slow and tedious process of hand labor, are now the results of the motive power of steam, while the functions of the workmen are limited to a superintendence which becomes almost a sinecure on account of the admirable precision and perfect execution of these machines.

---

gave out the silk-worm eggs to the laborers, upon the condition that a quintal (100 pounds) **of cocoons** be returned for every ounce of eggs; also, giving them a sufficient quantity of **mulberry leaves** to feed the worms hatched from the eggs, and a certain quantity more. The **cocoons** produced from the surplus constituted the profit of the silk-worm cultivators.

It is thus that fabrics, alike beautiful and useful, once ranked among articles of luxury, and accessible only to the wealthy, are each day rendered more available to the masses, contributing both to the prosperity of the producer and the gratification of the consumer. So far from despairing of ultimate success in rivalling the most elaborate and brilliant productions of Europe in this department of industry, the people of the United States may take courage from the fact that already a most successful beginning has been made in silk weaving.

Paterson, New Jersey, and Hartford, Manchester, and Mansfield, Connecticut, are already noted for their extensive silk manufactures.

For many years past all the sewing silk and twist used in the United States have been of home manufacture.[1] The same is, in a measure, true of pongee handkerchiefs. Rapid progress is being made in the weaving of ribbons, braids, trimmings, fringes, and various kinds of dress goods.

More especially may Americans be encouraged to prosecute this industry in view of the exemption of our continent from the malady among silk-worms now prevailing in Europe.

The devastation carried by the epidemic can hardly be overestimated. The steady advance of the malady threatens to embrace within its widening circles the silk-growing countries of the east, and thus cut off one of the main sources whence European manufacturers draw their supplies of raw material.

The calamity has thrown a pall over silk industry in all its branches. In the course of a speech on agriculture, delivered last year in the Corps Legislatif, M. Thiers said that the annual loss to silk culture in France from this cause alone, for several years, has been upwards of 100,000,000 of francs, ($20,000,000.)

Andrew Murray, esq., in an elaborate report on "Products of Useful Insects" at the Paris Exhibition, printed in the Illustrated London News of the 6th of July last, in speaking of the supply of *graines* (eggs) in the future, says:

"While things jog on as before from year to year, the cultivator will be slow to believe it possible that a time may come when no fresh *graines* (or eggs) are to be had. But the supply hangs upon a thread; when every silk country in the world shall have become infected, then the supply must cease. And we are not far from that stage. Japan and Australia are the only countries now free. When they go, the silk trade will collapse, and silk be blotted from the list of textile fabrics. That indeed would be a calamity which would come home to ourselves. Our silk spinners and silk weavers, our ribbon makers, our silk mercers, and the thousands who depend on these trades for subsistence, would have their occupation gone, and ruin and starvation would await a large portion of our population. Surely, to avert such a result, not only in this

---

[1] The Williams Silk Manufacturing Company, of New York, exhibited excellent "silk twist," for sewing machines, for which *honorable mention* was made, equivalent to a diploma.

country, (Great Britain,) but also over a large part of the continent, deserves that **every suggestion** which promises escape should be carefully considered; **and** surely, if **by** any measure, however stringent, one country could **be** cleansed from the infection before its spread ends in **a** complete extinction of the race, and so the threatened ruin averted, it ought to be adopted."

Unlike almost all epidemics, this does **not disappear from a** locality after one or two visitations, but once established, it remains, while its virulence increases rather than diminishes. This extraordinary trait is attributed to the fact that the silk-worm, by the law of its existence, is an annual, and therefore has no acclimated subjects, but presents to the epidemic a yearly supply of fresh victims. And **in** view of the geographical **position of** the United States, **it** may be noted, that M. de Quatrefages, **an** eminent French writer, **who** has carefully studied this subject, expresses **the opinion that, contrary** to the general course of epidemics, **this travels eastward rather** than westward.

This mysterious malady, which seems destined to destroy silk husbandry in the **whole** eastern hemisphere, has not appeared in the western. In view of its easterly course, and with the Pacific ocean between it and the American continent, **and with our** superior climatic conditions, it is hoped and believed that with precaution and care **it will** never reach our shores.

The soils, and especially the climate **of those** States of the Union where the cotton plant and **the sugar cane** have been wont to flourish, are peculiarly adapted to the **raising of the** mulberry and the **raising of** silk-worms.

From obvious causes some **of the long existing industries of portions of** these States will hereafter be **necessarily modified to a** noticeable **extent.** The culture of cotton and the production of sugar **will not so** exclusively engross the attention of their population as formerly. A portion **of** their capital and labor will doubtless seek new fields for the exercise **of their** energies.

Are **not these** facts an exhortation, an admonition even, to the people of the **United** States, to promptly avail themselves of their providential advantages, **and by** devoting a liberal share of their resources to the production and manufacture of silk, save this important and beautiful industry from **ruin, while at** the same time they advance the prosperity of their own **country and confer** incalculable blessings upon the world?

In conclusion, **the** undersigned cannot refrain from expressing here publicly his thanks **to** Messieurs Arles-Dufour and Duseigneur, of Lyons, **and M. Alcan, of** Paris, as well as to the many prominent manufacturers and merchants **in** the different centres of industry in Europe whom he has visited, for **their kindness in** assisting to make the numerous researches which became necessary in **the** examination of this important and diversified subject.

The works of M. Louis Reybaud, M. Pasteur, M. de Quatrefages, the archives **of** the chambers **of** commerce of the various cities of France,

Switzerland, and Germany, and especially that of Lyons, have been valuable sources of information.

The report now submitted has swelled far beyond the limits anticipated at its commencement; but, silk industry in all its branches, now grown to such importance throughout Europe, the conspicuous place it occupied in the Exposition; its comparative novelty in the United States, and the prospect that ere long it will be firmly established and diligently prosecuted in many sections of our country, seemed to call for a careful and thorough investigation, and a full and detailed statement of facts and conclusions.

I have the honor to be, sir, very respectfully, your obedient servant,

ELLIOT C. COWDIN.

Hon. WILLIAM H. SEWARD,
   Secretary of State, Washington, D. C.

INDEX.

www.ingramcontent.com/pod-product-compliance
Lightning Source LLC
Chambersburg PA
CBHW032117080426
42733CB00008B/971

* 9 7 8 3 7 4 3 3 0 9 8 4 5 *